NUTS

NUTS

NUTRITIOUS RECIPES WITH NUTS, FROM
SAVOURY TO SWEET

This edition published by Parragon Books Ltd in 2016
LOVE FOOD is an imprint of Parragon Books Ltd

Parragon Books Ltd
Chartist House
15–17 Trim Street
Bath BA1 1HA, UK
www.parragon.com/lovefood

ISBN 978-1-4748-1772-1

Printed in China

Cover photography by Tony Briscoe
New recipes, introduction and incidental text by Robin Donovan
New photography by Ian Garlick

Notes for the Reader
This book uses both metric and imperial measurements. Follow the same units of measurement throughout; do not mix metric and imperial. All spoon measurements are level: teaspoons are assumed to be 5 ml, and tablespoons are assumed to be 15 ml. Unless otherwise stated, milk is assumed to be full fat, eggs and individual vegetables are medium, pepper is freshly ground black pepper and salt is table salt. A pinch of salt is calculated as $1/16$ of a teaspoon. Unless otherwise stated, all root vegetables should be peeled prior to using.

The times given are an approximate guide only. Preparation times differ according to the techniques used by different people and the cooking times may also vary from those given.

While the author has made all reasonable efforts to ensure that the information contained in this book is accurate and up to date at the time of publication, anyone reading this book should note the following important points: -

Medical and pharmaceutical knowledge is constantly changing and the author and the publisher cannot and do not guarantee the accuracy or appropriateness of the contents of this book;
In any event, this book is not intended to be, and should not be relied upon, as a substitute for appropriate, tailored professional advice. Both the author and the publisher strongly recommend that a doctor or other healthcare professional is consulted before embarking on major dietary changes;
For the reasons set out above, and to the fullest extent permitted by law, the author and publisher: (i) cannot and do not accept any legal duty of care or responsibility in relation to the accuracy or appropriateness of the contents of this book, even where expressed as 'advice' or using other words to this effect; and (ii) disclaim any liability, loss, damage or risk that may be claimed or incurred as a consequence – directly or indirectly – of the use and/or application of any of the contents of this book.

CONTENTS

INTRODUCTION

What is a nut? Botanically speaking, a nut is a hard-shelled pod that contains a single seed and doesn't open when the fruit is mature. These include chestnuts, hazelnuts and acorns. But in the culinary world, the word nut has a much broader definition, including certain drupes (a fruit with flesh surrounding a shell or a stone with a single seed inside), such as walnuts, almonds, pecan nuts, macadamia nuts and coconuts; some legumes, which grow in multi-seed pods that split open to reveal the seeds, such as peanuts; and various other seeds such as pine nuts, cashew nuts and Brazil nuts. For our purposes, these are all nuts.

Nuts in all their variety may be the most underrated heroes of the food world. There's no denying that these little morsels are delicious – whether eaten on their own or tossed into salads, stirred into biscuit dough, baked into muffins or cakes, or sprinkled over ice cream, yogurt or porridge. Part of their lure is their versatility – they can be eaten raw or toasted, whole or chopped, or can be ground into flours or butters. What's more, you can carry them with you wherever you go, and they have a really long shelf life.

Adding to their superpowers, nuts are also absolutely packed with nutrition – they are full of the protein, fibre, vitamins, minerals and healthy monounsaturated and polyunsaturated fats that help you curb your appetite, protect against heart disease, lower cholesterol and reduce your risk of developing cancer.

If you're a vegetarian or vegan, nuts can be an especially important part of your healthy diet since they are a great source of protein and one of the best plant-based sources of healthy fats. Nut butters, especially, are a great way to get quick protein when you don't eat meat.

In short, nuts – ranging from almonds, walnuts and hazelnuts to cashews, Brazil nuts and pistachios – will benefit both your health and your palate. So what are you waiting for? Experiment with some of the recipes shown here and both your taste buds and your body will thank you.

BRAZIL NUT

MACADAMIA NUT

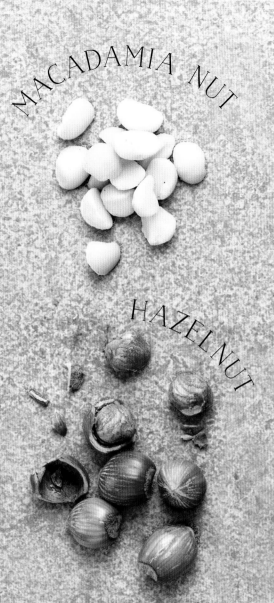

HAZELNUT

CASHEW NUT

CHESTNUT

ALMOND

PINE NUT

WALNUT

PECAN

PEANUT

PISTACHIO

SPREADS & SNACKS

Maple & Cinnamon Cashew Butter	12
Vanilla & Macadamia Nut Butter	14
Roasted Almond Gingersnap Butter	16
Pumpkin Pecan Butter	18
Spicy Chilli & Lime Peanut Butter	20
Home-made Cacao & Hazelnut Butter	22
NUT BUTTERS	24
Five-spice Cashews	26
Chewy Apricot & Almond Energy Bars	28
Walnut & Linseed Crackers	30
Plain Chocolate & Peanut Butter Energy Balls	32
Pecan Oatcakes	34
Raw Date & Coconut Bars	36
Mixed Nuts in Herbed Salt	38

MAPLE & CINNAMON CASHEW BUTTER

Super creamy, just a little sweet and with a kick of cinnamon, this rich spread is simply delicious on toast or apple wedges, as a sandwich filling, or for any little treat where you'd normally enjoy a dollop of ready-made peanut butter.

MAKES: 375 g/13 oz   **PREP TIME:** 5 mins   **COOK TIME:** none

INGREDIENTS

250 g/9 oz roasted unsalted cashew nuts

3 tbsp maple syrup

1 tsp vanilla extract

¾ tsp cinnamon

pinch of salt

2 tsp coconut oil

1. Place the nuts in a food processor and process for 1 minute. Scrape down the side of the bowl and process again for 1–2 minutes. Repeat the process until you have a smooth paste.

2. Add the maple syrup, vanilla extract, cinnamon and salt and continue processing until the mixture is very smooth. With the processor running, add the oil and process until well combined.

3. Serve immediately or store in a covered container in the refrigerator for several weeks.

per 375 g/13 oz: 1685 Kcals / 124.9g fat / 30.7g sat fat / 124g carbs / 49.4g sugars / 8.5g protein / 38.4g fibre / 1.6g salt

VANILLA & MACADAMIA NUT BUTTER

Macadamia nuts are rich in flavour and have a creamy texture. Because of their high oil content, they become quite runny when ground. Cashew nuts are milder in flavour but sturdier in consistency when ground and provide good structure, making it very spreadable.

MAKES: 225 g/9¾ oz   **PREP TIME:** 5 mins   **COOK TIME:** none

INGREDIENTS

135 g/4¾ oz roasted, unsalted macadamia nuts

120 g/4¼ oz roasted, unsalted cashew nuts

1 tsp vanilla extract

¼ tsp salt

1. Put the macadamia nuts and cashew nuts into a food processor and process for 3–4 minutes until very smooth.

2. Add the vanilla extract and salt and process to incorporate. Serve immediately or transfer to a covered container and store in the refrigerator for up to 3 weeks.

per 225 g/9¾ oz: 1670 Kcals / 158.3g fat / 27.1g sat fat / 57.8g carbs / 12.1g sugars / 14.4g fibre / 28.9g protein / 1.5g salt

ROASTED ALMOND GINGERSNAP BUTTER

Lightly sweetened with treacle and brown sugar and spiced with both fresh and ground ginger, this healthy nut butter tastes just like ground up gingersnaps. Try it spread on crisp apples or on toast with sliced pears.

MAKES: 350 g/12 oz   **PREP TIME:** 10 mins   **COOK TIME:** none

INGREDIENTS

285 g/10¼ oz roasted almonds

2 tbsp soft light brown sugar

2 tbsp black treacle

1½ tsp grated fresh ginger

½ tsp ground ginger

¼ tsp salt

2–3 tbsp grapeseed oil

1. Put the almonds into a food processor and process for 5–10 minutes, until smooth.

2. Add the sugar, treacle, fresh ginger, ground ginger, and salt and process until well combined. With the processor running, add the oil, a little at a time, until you achieve the desired consistency.

3. Serve immediately or refrigerate until ready to use. Almond butter can be stored in the refrigerator for several weeks.

TIP: *It can take a while for almonds to release their oils so that your almond butter has the right consistency. Keep processing until you get a smooth, creamy paste.*

per 350 g/12 oz: 2204 Kcals / 182.3g fat / 14.8g sat fat / 110.5g carbs / 63g sugars / 31.2g fibre / 60.5g protein / 1.5g salt

PUMPKIN PECAN BUTTER

This smoothly satisfying tasty butter offers everything you love about pumpkin pie filling but in a spread that's perfect on toast, crusty bread, muffins or slices of fruit.

MAKES: 500 g/1 lb 2 oz   **PREP TIME:** 5 mins   **COOK TIME:** 8–10 mins

INGREDIENTS

55 g/2 oz pecan nuts, chopped

6 tbsp soft light brown sugar

425 g/15 oz canned pumpkin purée

1 tbsp black treacle

½ tsp ground cinnamon

½ tsp ground allspice

⅛ tsp ground cloves

⅛ tsp ground nutmeg

¼ tsp salt

1. Put the nuts into a food processor and process for 2–3 minutes until smooth. Scrape the mixture into a medium-sized saucepan.

2. Add the remaining ingredients and bring to the boil over a medium–high heat. Reduce the heat to low and cook for 8–10 minutes, stirring frequently, until the mixture darkens and becomes very thick.

3. Leave to cool to room temperature.

4. Serve immediately or store in a covered container in the refrigerator for up to 1 week.

per 500 g/1 lb 2 oz: 923 Kcals / 41g fat / 4.1g sat fat / 142.9g carbs / 115.3g sugars / 18.7g fibre / 10g protein / 1.6g salt

SPICY CHILLI & LIME PEANUT BUTTER

This sweet and spicy peanut butter will change the way you think of the humble peanut-butter sandwich forever. Try it slathered between slices of toasted wholemeal bread with a slice of ripe tomato, crunchy cucumber and a crisp lettuce leaf.

MAKES: 250 g/9 oz   **PREP TIME:** 5 mins   **COOK TIME:** none

INGREDIENTS

225 g/8 oz roasted, unsalted peanuts

½ tsp cayenne pepper

¼ tsp salt

grated zest and juice of 1 lime

1 tsp soft light brown sugar

1 tbsp coconut oil

1. Put the peanuts into a food processor and process for 2–3 minutes until smooth. Add the cayenne pepper, salt, lime zest and juice and sugar and process until well combined.

2. With the machine running, add the oil and process until the mixture is smooth and well incorporated. Serve immediately or transfer to a jar and store in the refrigerator for several weeks.

TIP: *This savoury butter makes a great sauce for pasta or noodles. Toss a few tablespoons of the butter, with a splash of the noodle cooking water, with hot spaghetti or rice noodles. Add shredded cooked chicken or diced tofu, and garnish with chopped fresh coriander and sliced spring onions.*

per 250 g /9 oz: 1510 Kcals / 125.5g fat / 27.3g sat fat / 68g carbs / 25.1g sugars / 18.8g fibre / 53.7g protein / 1.5g salt

HOME-MADE CACAO & HAZELNUT BUTTER

This delicious nut butter, made with wholesome ingredients and some sweetness thrown in, is a beautifully satisfying treat when spread on wholegrain toast or hot pancakes.

MAKES: 225 g/8 oz   **PREP TIME:** 15 mins   **COOK TIME:** 3–4 mins

INGREDIENTS

115 g/4 oz unblanched hazelnuts

25 g/1 oz raw cacao powder

65 g/2½ oz light muscovado sugar

125 ml/4 fl oz light olive oil

½ tsp natural vanilla extract

pinch of sea salt

1. Add the hazelnuts to a dry frying pan and cook over a medium heat for 3–4 minutes, constantly shaking the pan, until the nuts are an even golden brown in colour.

2. Wrap the nuts in a clean tea towel and rub to remove the skins.

3. Put the nuts into a blender and blend until finely ground. Add the cacao powder, sugar, oil, vanilla extract and salt, and blend again to make a smooth paste. Spoon into a small preserving jar and clip the lid in place. Leave to stand at room temperature for 4 hours, until the sugar has dissolved completely. Stir again, then store in the refrigerator for up to 5 days.

per 225 g/8 oz: 430 Kcals / 40g fat / 5.2g sat fat / 19.5g carbs / 13.9g sugars / 4g fibre / 4.1g protein / 0.3g salt

NUT BUTTERS

You can buy a jar of peanut butter or almond butter in any supermarket, but in just a few minutes and at a fraction of the cost, you can make your own luscious – and far more exotic – nut butters in your own kitchen. Once you understand the essentials of making a basic nut butter, you'll then be free to experiment and introduce different flavour combinations.

The flavour possibilities for home-made nut butters are extensive, from macadamia–roasted almond, hazelnut–chocolate, cashew–cinnamon to maple–pecan – the list just goes on.

Making nut butters couldn't be simpler. The only equipment you need is a good food processor or a high-speed blender. Add in a handful of nuts and whatever additions you'd like – think honey, maple syrup, cocoa powder, ground cinnamon or other spices, raisins, sultanas or other dried fruits, chocolate chips, anything you fancy – will quickly be transformed into a delectable nut butter.

These delightful spreads can dress up a plain piece of toast, but they also make a fantastic dip for fresh fruit, a great filling for sandwiches or a delicious spread for cookies. You could add some to biscuit dough or cake batter for extra flavour, or swirl it into brownie or muffin batter just before baking. A savoury butter also makes a delicious sauce when tossed with hot noodles or pasta or drizzled over cooked vegetables.

HERE'S HOW:

1. Place the nuts in your food processor or blender.

2. Pulse several times to grind the nuts. If you prefer a chunky nut butter, remove a small portion of the nuts now and reserve them to add back in later.

3. Process for 1 minute, scrape down the side and base of the bowl, and process again for 1 minute. Repeat until the mixture is very smooth and creamy.

4. Add salt, oil, sweeteners or other flavourings. Process for a further 2–3 minutes until the mixture is very smooth. If you've reserved some roughly chopped nuts, or if you're using other ingredients such as chocolate chips, add them now and pulse to incorporate.

5. Enjoy!

TOP 5 TIPS FOR MAKING HOME-MADE NUT BUTTERS

1. Use a powerful food processor or high-speed blender.

2. For the best flavour and texture, toast your nuts just before processing.

3. Be patient. It takes a while, but if you process your nuts for long enough you'll experience a magical moment when they transform into a creamy and utterly divine spread.

4. For added creaminess and cohesiveness, add a little oil – peanut, coconut or grapeseed oils are ideal.

5. Be creative! Use a combination of nuts and add different sweeteners, spices, extracts or other ingredients. The possibilities are endless.

FIVE-SPICE CASHEWS

Peppercorns, star anise, fennel, cloves and cinnamon combine here with the natural sweetness of cashews. For a moreish snack or a pre-dinner or barbecue appetizer with a spicy character, this nutty concoction performs at every level.

SERVES: 8   **PREP TIME:** 5 mins   **COOK TIME:** 10–12 mins

INGREDIENTS

1 tbsp groundnut oil, for oiling

½ tsp Szechuan peppercorns

2 star anise pods

½ tsp fennel seeds

6 whole cloves

½ tsp ground cinnamon

2 tbsp water

50 g/1¾ oz soft light brown sugar

1 tsp salt

250 g/9 oz toasted, unsalted cashew nuts

1. Preheat the oven to 200°C/400°F/Gas Mark 6. Lightly oil a baking tray and a large piece of foil.

2. In a spice grinder, grind together the peppercorns, star anise pods, fennel seeds and cloves until finely ground. Add the cinnamon and mix well.

3. Put the water and sugar into a medium-sized saucepan and heat over a medium heat, stirring constantly, for 2 minutes, or until the sugar is dissolved. Add the spice mixture and salt and stir to mix well. Add the nuts and stir to coat completely. Cook, stirring, for a further minute.

4. Transfer the nuts to the prepared tin and spread out in an even layer. Roast in the preheated oven for 6–8 minutes until most of the liquid has evaporated. Transfer the nuts to the prepared foil and separate them so that they don't stick together. Leave to cool completely before serving.

5. Store in an airtight container at room temperature for up to 2 weeks.

per serving: 219 Kcals / 16.2g fat / 3.2g sat fat / 16.6g carbs / 7.6g sugars / 1.1g fibre / 4.8g protein / 1.8g salt

3

4

CHEWY APRICOT & ALMOND ENERGY BARS

These flapjack-style, dairy-free energy bars are full of fruit and fibre and, when you have a supply in the cupboard, are a first-rate choice for a portable, healthy mid-morning snack.

MAKES: 15   **PREP TIME:** 25 mins   **COOK TIME:** 30 mins

INGREDIENTS

115 g/4 oz coconut oil

85 g/3 oz light muscovado sugar

60 g/2¼ oz almond butter, or other nut butter

1 dessert apple, cored and roughly grated

150 g/5½ oz porridge oats

40 g/1½ oz brown rice flour

55 g/2 oz unblanched almonds, roughly chopped

40 g/1½ oz sunflower seeds

200 g/7 oz dried apricots, diced

1. Preheat the oven to 180°C/350°F/Gas Mark 4. Line a 20-cm/8-inch shallow square cake tin with non-stick baking paper.

2. Heat the oil and sugar in a medium-sized saucepan over a low heat until the oil has melted and the sugar is dissolved. Remove from the heat and stir in the almond butter, until melted.

3. Add the apple, oats, flour, almonds and sunflower seeds, and mix together well.

4. Spoon two thirds of the mixture into the prepared tin and press down firmly. Sprinkle over the apricots and press firmly into the base layer, then dot the remaining oat mixture over the top in a thin layer so that some of the apricots are still visible.

5. Bake in the preheated oven for about 25 minutes, until the top is golden brown. Remove from the oven and leave to cool in the tin until almost cold, then cut into 15 small rectangles. Leave to cool completely, then lift the bars out of the tin, using the paper. Separate the bars and pack into a plastic container. Store in the refrigerator for up to 3 days.

per bar: 235 Kcals / 14g fat / 7.2g sat fat / 26.6g carbs / 14.6g sugars / 3.5g fibre / 4.2g protein/ trace salt

WALNUT & LINSEED CRACKERS

Walnuts and linseeds combine in a cracker to create a nutritional powerhouse. Walnuts, one of the most health-giving nuts, include omega-3 fats, amino acids and antioxidants, and linseeds are a rich source of micronutrients, manganese and vitamin B1.

MAKES: 40   **PREP TIME:** 20 mins, plus chilling   **COOK TIME:** 22 mins

INGREDIENTS

70 g/2½ oz ground linseeds

150 g/5½ oz wholemeal flour

½ tsp salt

2 tbsp soft light brown sugar

85 g/3 oz unsalted butter, at room temperature

125 ml/4 fl oz milk

145 g/5¼ oz raisins

60 g/2¼ oz walnuts, chopped

35 g/1¼ oz whole linseeds

10 g/¼ oz wholemeal flour, for dusting

1. Preheat the oven to 180°C/350°F/Gas Mark 4. Put the ground linseeds, flour, salt and sugar into a large mixing bowl and mix with a hand-held electric mixer. Add the butter and mix on medium speed for 2–3 minutes until coarse crumbs form.

2. Add the milk, raisins, walnuts and whole linseeds and mix until the dough comes together. Turn out the dough onto a piece of clingfilm and shape it into a round. Wrap in the clingfilm and chill in the refrigerator for about 10 minutes.

3. Lay a large sheet of baking paper on a work surface. Turn out the dough onto the paper and flatten it into a large rectangle with the palms of your hands. Sprinkle with a little flour, then roll out as thinly as possible (to the thickness of the chopped nuts).

4. Using a sharp knife, score the dough into 5-cm/2-inch squares. Slide the paper onto a large baking sheet and bake in the preheated oven for 20–22 minutes, until the crackers are lightly browned. Remove from the oven, break the crackers apart and leave to cool before serving.

per cracker: 68 Kcals / 4g fat / 1.4g sat fat / 7.6g carbs / 3.1g sugars / 1.4g fibre / 1.5g protein / 0.1g salt

1

2

3

PLAIN CHOCOLATE & PEANUT BUTTER ENERGY BALLS

Energy balls typically combine protein, carbohydrates and fats in a handy, portable shape. Chocolate with more than 80 per cent cocoa is used here as a powdered coating – another option would be to roll the balls in powdered cinnamon.

MAKES: 8   **PREP TIME:** 15 mins, plus chilling   **COOK TIME:** none

INGREDIENTS

50 g/1¾ oz almond flour

60 g/2¼ oz unsweetened peanut butter

20 g/¾ oz unsalted peanuts, roughly chopped

3 tbsp flaxseeds

30 g/1 oz plain chocolate with 85% cocoa, finely chopped

1 tsp cocoa powder

sea salt (optional)

1. Put the almond flour in a food processor and process for a minute, until you have the texture of rough flour.

2. Put the peanut butter, peanuts, flaxseeds, chocolate and a small pinch of salt, if using, in a bowl and mix. Add the almond flour, reserving 1½ tablespoons. Mix until you have a texture resembling chunky clay.

3. Sprinkle the remaining almond flour and the cocoa powder onto a plate and mix with a teaspoon. Form a tablespoon-sized blob of the peanut mixture into a ball using your palms. Roll it in the cocoa powder mixture, then transfer to a plate. Make a further seven balls in the same way.

4. Cover and chill in the refrigerator for at least 30 minutes, or up to two days.

> **TIP:** *If the coating of cocoa powder is too bitter and strong for your taste, substitute it with a teaspoon of ground cinnamon.*

per ball: 144 Kcals / 11.9g fat / 2.1g sat fat / 5.9g carbs / 1.7g sugars / 3.0g fibre / 4.9g protein / 0.3g salt

PECAN OATCAKES

These Scottish-style oatcakes are studded with crunchy chopped pecan nuts, giving them a nutty flavour and added texture. They make the perfect accompaniment to a cheese plate, or you could eat them on their own as a simple snack.

MAKES: 40   **PREP TIME:** 20 mins   **COOK TIME:** 15 mins

INGREDIENTS

90 g/3¼ oz porridge oats

125 g/4½ oz plain flour

¾ tsp sugar

½ tsp bicarbonate of soda

¼ tsp salt

115 g/4 oz chilled unsalted butter, cut into small pieces

3 tbsp water

50 g/1¾ oz pecan nuts, chopped

10 g/¼ oz plain flour, for dusting

1. Preheat the oven to 190°C/375°F/Gas Mark 5.

2. Put the oats, flour, sugar, bicarbonate of soda and salt into a food processor. Add the butter and pulse until the mixture resembles coarse crumbs. With the processor running, slowly add the water and process until the mixture comes together in a thick dough. Add the nuts and pulse until they are just incorporated.

3. Turn out the dough onto a sheet of baking paper and lightly dust with flour. Using a lightly floured rolling pin, roll out the dough to a very thin rectangle. Score the dough into 5-cm/2-inch squares with a sharp knife.

4. Transfer the squares on the paper to a baking sheet and bake in the preheated oven for 13–15 minutes until light brown and crisp. Remove from the oven and transfer on the paper to a wire rack. Leave to cool completely before removing from the paper. Serve at room temperature.

per oatcake: 53 Kcals / 3.4g fat / 1.6g sat fat / 4.3g carbs / 0.2g sugars / 0.4g fibre / 0.8g protein / 0.1g salt

RAW DATE & COCONUT BARS

These chunky, nutty bars get the most out of power-packed raw ingredients.
They are the perfect way of keeping you energized throughout the afternoon.

MAKES: 12   **PREP TIME:** 30 mins   **COOK TIME:** none

INGREDIENTS

400 g/14 oz Medjool dates, halved and stoned

60 g/2¼ oz unblanched almonds

60 g/2¼ oz cashew nut pieces

35 g/1¼ oz chia seeds

2 tbsp maca (powdered superfood)

2 tsp natural vanilla extract

20 g/¾ oz desiccated coconut

55 g/2 oz unblanched hazelnuts, roughly chopped

25 g/1 oz pecan nuts, broken in half

1. Add the dates, almonds and cashew pieces to a food processor and process until finely chopped.

2. Add the chia seeds, maca and vanilla extract, and process until the mixture binds together in a rough ball.

3. Tear off two sheets of non-stick baking paper, put one on the work surface and sprinkle with half the coconut. Put the date ball on top then press into a roughly-shaped rectangle with your fingertips. Cover with the second sheet of paper and roll out to a 30 x 20-cm/12 x 8-inch rectangle. Lift off the top piece of paper, sprinkle with the remaining coconut, the hazelnuts and pecan nuts, then recover with the paper and briefly roll with a rolling pin to press the nuts into the date mixture.

4. Loosen the top paper, then transfer the date mixture, still on the base paper, to a tray and chill for 3 hours or overnight, until firm.

5. Remove the top paper, cut the date mixture into 12 pieces, peel off the base paper then pack into a plastic container, layering with pieces of baking paper to keep them separate. Store in the refrigerator for up to 3 days.

per bar: 225 Kcals / 11g fat / 2g sat fat / 31.7g carbs / 23.5g sugars / 5.4g fibre / 4.2g protein / trace salt

MIXED NUTS
IN HERBED SALT

Simple to make and wonderfully tasty, these moreish pan-roasted nuts are bursting with protein, healthy fats and lots of flavour.

SERVES: 4   **PREP TIME:** 5 mins, plus cooling   **COOK TIME:** 5 mins

INGREDIENTS

1 tbsp olive oil

2 fresh rosemary sprigs, leaves torn from stems

55 g/2 oz cashew nuts

55 g/2 oz pecan nuts

55 g/2 oz unblanched almonds

55 g/2 oz unblanched hazelnuts

½ tsp sea salt

1. Heat the oil and rosemary in a medium frying pan, then swirl the oil around the pan to infuse with the rosemary. Add the nuts and cook over a medium heat for 2–3 minutes, until lightly toasted.

2. Stir in the salt, then spoon the nuts into a bowl and leave to cool before eating. Any leftover nuts can be stored in the refrigerator in a plastic container or preserving jar for up to 3 days.

TIP: *Instead of rosemary, try replacing with a little curry powder or a blend of ground turmeric, garam masala, smoked paprika and a pinch of chilli.*

per serving: 366 Kcals / 34.4g fat / 3.5g sat fat / 11.3g carbs / 2.5g sugars / 4.8g fibre / 8.7g protein / 0.7g salt

BREAKFAST & BRUNCH

VANILLA, ALMOND & BANANA SMOOTHIE

This almond-based smoothie is sweetened only with dates, but it tastes as sweet and delicious as the best milkshake you ever had – it is also packed with protein!

SERVES: 2   **PREP TIME:** 5 mins   **COOK TIME:** 5 mins

INGREDIENTS

225 ml/8 fl oz almond milk

60 g/2¼ oz almond butter

1 banana

4 stoned dates

1 tsp vanilla extract

8–10 ice cubes

1. Place all of the ingredients in a blender and blend on high speed until smooth.

2. Pour into two glasses and serve immediately.

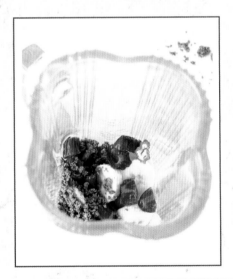

TIP: *When buying almond milk, choose one made with just almonds and water if possible. Some ready-made varieties have added sugar and are very sweet.*

per serving: 330 Kcals / 18.1g fat / 1.4g sat fat / 31.4g carbs / 24.4g sugars / 6.4g fibre / 9.4g protein / 0.2g salt

PROTEIN BERRY WHIP

Frozen berries are a healthy and handy storecupboard staple.
Blitz with protein-boosting cashew and Brazil nuts for a delicious shake.

SERVES: 4   **PREP TIME:** 10–15 mins   **COOK TIME:** none

INGREDIENTS

250 g/9 oz frozen
mixed sliced strawberries
and blueberries

40 g/1½ oz Brazil nuts

40 g/1½ oz cashew
nut pieces

25 g/1 oz porridge oats

450 ml/15 fl oz
almond milk

2 tbsp maple syrup

1. Place the frozen berries, Brazil nuts and cashew nuts in a blender. Sprinkle over the oats, then pour in half the almond milk. Blend until smooth.

2. Add the remaining milk and maple syrup, and blend again until smooth. Pour into four glasses and serve immediately with spoons. As the drink stands, the blueberries will almost set the liquid, but as soon as you stir it, it will turn to liquid again.

per serving: 213 Kcals / 12.8g fat / 2.4g sat fat / 23.2g carbs / 11.6g sugars / 3.5g fibre / 4.7g protein / 0.2g salt

1

2

3

PEANUT BUTTER & BANANA PANCAKES

Peanut butter and banana is a time-honoured combination, and for good reason. Here, the dynamic duo flavours fluffy pancakes, finished off with a rich and decadent peanut butter-infused maple syrup.

SERVES: 4   **PREP TIME:** 20 mins, plus standing   **COOK TIME:** 15 mins

INGREDIENTS

140 g/5 oz roasted, unsalted peanuts

90 g/3¼ oz wholemeal flour

90 g/3¼ oz plain flour

2 tbsp soft light brown sugar

2 tsp baking powder

pinch of salt

2 ripe bananas

350 ml/12 fl oz milk

2 eggs

2 tbsp butter

175 ml/6 fl oz maple syrup

1. Put the peanuts into a food processor and process for 2–3 minutes until smooth.

2. Put the wholemeal flour, plain flour, sugar, baking powder and salt into a medium-sized mixing bowl. Put 1 banana into a separate large mixing bowl, mash well, then add the milk, eggs and half the peanut butter and stir until well combined. Add the dry mixture to the wet mixture and mix with a hand-held electric mixer until well combined, adding a little more milk if needed. Leave to stand for 5 minutes.

3. Thinly slice the remaining banana.

4. Heat 1 tablespoon of the butter in a large frying pan over a medium–high heat. Add the batter, 6 tablespoons at a time, and top each pancake with 3–5 banana slices, pressing them into the batter. Cook for 2–3 minutes until bubbles form and begin to burst on top of the pancakes. Flip the pancakes over and cook for a further 1–2 minutes, until golden brown. Repeat with the remaining batter, adding additional butter to the pan as needed.

5. Meanwhile, combine the maple syrup and the remaining peanut butter in a small saucepan and heat over a medium heat, stirring frequently, until hot and well combined. Keep warm until ready to serve.

6. Serve the pancakes hot, drizzled with the syrup.

per serving: 700 Kcals / 29.3g fat / 8.6g sat fat / 96.1g carbs / 47.2g sugars / 7.3g fibre / 20.2g protein / 1.3g salt

VANILLA & BERRY OVERNIGHT PORRIDGE

Porridge for breakfast doesn't get any easier than this. Combine oats and milk before you go to bed and when you wake up in the morning, breakfast is ready! There are endless possible variations on this simple and satisfying breakfast.

SERVES: 2   **PREP TIME:** 5 mins, plus chilling   **COOK TIME:** none

INGREDIENTS

50 g/1¾ oz porridge oats

150 ml/5 fl oz unsweetened almond milk

½ tsp vanilla extract

2 tsp honey

4 tbsp low-fat vanilla yogurt

35 g/1¼ oz blueberries

40 g/1½ oz strawberries, sliced

1 tbsp toasted sliced almonds

1. Place the oats in a serving bowl. Pour over the almond milk and add the vanilla extract and honey. Stir, cover and refrigerate for at least 4 hours or overnight.

2. Remove the mixture from the refrigerator, add the yogurt and stir well. Top with the blueberries, strawberries and almonds and serve immediately.

TIP: *Substitute any type of milk – cow's, coconut, cashew, rice, soy etc. Or vary the flavour with different fresh or dried fruits, nuts, or by adding natural sweeteners, such as maple syrup or agave nectar.*

---

per serving: 199 Kcals / 5.5g fat / 0.8g sat fat / 31.9g carbs / 13.2g sugars / 4g fibre / 6.2g protein / 0.1g salt

YOGURT WITH BLUEBERRIES, HONEY & NUTS

Greek yogurt topped with fresh berries, honey and nuts is a magical combination and a quick and delicious breakfast treat.

SERVES: 4   **PREP TIME:** 10 mins   **COOK TIME:** 5 mins

INGREDIENTS

3 tbsp clear honey

85 g/3 oz mixed unsalted nuts

8 tbsp Greek-style yogurt

200 g/7 oz fresh blueberries

1. Heat the honey in a small saucepan over medium heat.

2. Add the nuts and stir until they are well coated. Remove from the heat and leave to cool slightly.

3. Divide the yogurt between four serving bowls, then spoon over the nut mixture and the blueberries and serve immediately.

per serving: 225 Kcals / 11.9g fat / 1.8g sat fat / 27.7g carbs / 21g sugars / 3.1g fibre / 5.8g protein / trace salt

SPICED QUINOA BREAKFAST BOWL WITH PECAN NUTS

Quinoa is packed with protein, making it a fantastic grain to include in a healthy breakfast. Here it's combined with zingy spices, sweet pears and crunchy nuts for a breakfast that is worth getting out of bed for.

SERVES: 2   **PREP TIME:** 15 mins   **COOK TIME:** 15 mins

INGREDIENTS

55 g/2 oz uncooked quinoa, rinsed well

150 ml/5 fl oz water

¼ tsp ground cinnamon

¼ tsp nutmeg

¼ tsp allspice

pinch of salt

4 tsp maple syrup

125 ml/4 fl oz almond milk

1 pear, cored and diced

35 g/1¼ oz pecan nuts, toasted

1. In small saucepan, combine the quinoa with the water, cinnamon, nutmeg, allspice and salt and bring to the boil over a medium–high heat. Reduce the heat to low, cover and simmer for about 15 minutes, until the quinoa is tender.

2. Stir in the maple syrup and divide the mixture between two serving bowls. Pour the almond milk over the top, dividing equally, and garnish with the pear pieces and pecan nuts. Serve immediately.

per serving: 320 Kcals / 15.5g fat / 1.4g sat fat / 42.9g carbs / 17.3g sugars / 6.8g fibre / 6.1g protein / 0.8g salt

HEALTH-GIVING NUTS

The reputed ability of nuts to reduce the risk of developing cancer is the attribute that really consolidates their designation as a superfood. However, they have other nutrients that give them an enviable reputation as a health powerhouse. Unsaturated fats (also referred to as 'good fats') – both monounsaturated and polyunsaturated – can help lower bad cholesterol levels, while omega-3 fatty acids help protect you from heart attacks. Incorporating nuts into your daily diet is an easy, and tasty, way to boost your health:

ALMONDS

Almonds are high in vitamin E, vitamin B and magnesium, which help to shore up your immune system. They also contain more fibre than any other nut, which can help you curb your appetite and control your blood sugar.

CASHEW NUTS

Cashew nuts contain loads of iron and zinc, which help carry oxygen to your cells, prevent anaemia, boost your immune system and support healthy vision. With the added bonus of a high dose of magnesium, a daily serving of these nuts could help improve your memory and protect against age-related memory loss.

BRAZIL NUTS

Brazil nuts are high in selenium, a mineral that may protect against bone, prostate and breast cancers.

CHESTNUTS

Chestnuts have a generous quantity of B vitamins that help produce red blood cells; break down protein, carbs and fats for energy; give you healthy skin; and boost brain function.

HAZELNUTS

Hazelnuts are rich in vitamin E, which can help prevent cataracts and macular degeneration, maintain healthy skin and reduce the risk of dementia.

MACADAMIA NUTS

Macadamia nuts are calorie-dense, but they also deliver the highest levels of heart-healthy monounsaturated fats, which help to lower cholesterol and blood pressure.

PEANUTS

Peanuts are a great source of copper, an essential mineral for red blood cell formation and for building a healthy immune system, blood vessels and bones.

PECAN NUTS

Pecans are loaded with antioxidants, which help prevent dangerous plaque build-up in your arteries.

PINE NUTS

Pine nuts contain high levels of vitamins A and lutein, which support healthy vision. Their high vitamin D content helps to build strong bones and teeth.

PISTACHIO NUTS

Pistachios are high in gamma-tocopherol, a type of vitamin E that may play a role in reducing lung cancer risk. Loaded with potassium and vitamin B6, they can help keep your nervous system and muscles healthy, boost your mood and bolster your immune system.

WALNUTS

Walnuts beat all other nuts for high levels of antioxidants, which protect your body from the type of cellular damage that can lead to heart disease, cancer and premature ageing. They're also an aid to reducing the high levels of stress that can lead to illness and a depressed immune system.

SWEET POTATO PANCAKES & CINNAMON CASHEW CREAM

Shredded sweet potato pancakes topped with a lightly sweetened cashew cream make a nutritious and satisfying breakfast or brunch.

SERVES: 4   PREP TIME: 15 mins, plus soaking   COOK TIME: 40 mins

INGREDIENTS

CASHEW CREAM

130 g/4¾ oz unsalted cashew nuts, soaked overnight, drained and rinsed

125 ml/4 fl oz water

2 tbsp maple syrup

½ tsp cinnamon

pinch of salt

PANCAKES

2 sweet potatoes, peeled and roughly grated

2 tbsp flour

pinch of salt

2 large eggs, lightly beaten

2 tbsp sunflower oil, for frying

1. To make the cashew cream, place the nuts in a blender with the water. Blend on medium speed, scraping down the side of the blender as needed, for 3–5 minutes until the nuts are puréed to a very smooth consistency. Add the maple syrup, cinnamon and salt and process on high speed until the mixture is smooth and well combined.

2. To make the pancakes, combine the sweet potatoes, flour and salt in a large mixing bowl, tossing to mix well. Add the eggs and mix well.

3. Heat 1 tablespoon of the oil in a large frying pan over a medium–high heat. Scoop the sweet potato mixture into the pan, using 125 ml/4 fl oz of mixture for each pancake. Flatten the pancakes slightly with the back of the spoon as you put them in the pan. Cover and cook for about 5 minutes until the pancakes are brown underneath. Flip over and cook, covered, for a further 5 minutes to brown the other side.

4. Repeat with the remaining batter, adding more oil as needed. Serve hot, with a drizzle of the cashew cream.

per serving: 401 Kcals / 24.1g fat / 4.2g sat fat / 37.5g carbs / 11.7g sugars / 4g fibre / 11.6g protein / 1g salt

2

1

3

CARROT CAKE MUFFINS

These sweet treats pack a healthy enough punch to make them a perfectly reasonable breakfast option. Full of nutrient-rich carrots, raisins and walnuts, and sweetened with brown sugar and apple sauce, they will make you happy at any time of day.

MAKES: 12   **PREP TIME:** 15 mins   **COOK TIME:** 22 mins

INGREDIENTS

10 g/¼ oz butter, for greasing

90 g/3¼ oz wholemeal flour

60 g/2¼ oz plain flour

1 tsp bicarbonate of soda

1½ tsp cinnamon

½ tsp ground ginger

½ tsp salt

165 g/5¾ oz soft light brown sugar

125 ml/4 fl oz unsweetened apple sauce

4 tbsp sunflower oil

1 tsp vanilla extract

2 eggs, at room temperature

2 carrots, finely grated

35 g/1¼ oz raisins

25 g/1 oz walnuts, chopped

1. Preheat the oven to 180°C/350°F/Gas Mark 4 and grease a 12-hole muffin tin.

2. Put the wholemeal flour, plain flour, bicarbonate of soda, cinnamon, ginger and salt into a medium-sized bowl and mix to combine.

3. Put the sugar, apple sauce and oil into a separate bowl and beat with a hand-held electric mixer until well combined. Add the vanilla extract and then add the eggs, one at a time, beating well after each addition.

4. Add the dry mixture to the wet mixture and beat for 1 minute until just combined. Gently stir in the carrots, raisins and walnuts. Scoop the batter into the prepared tin.

5. Bake in the preheated oven for 20–22 minutes, or until a cocktail stick inserted into the centre of a muffin comes out clean. Leave to cool in the tin for a few minutes, then transfer the muffins to a wire rack and leave to cool completely. Serve warm or at room temperature.

per muffin: 187 Kcals / 7.6g fat / 1.3g sat fat / 27.8g carbs / 16.7g sugars / 1.8g fibre / 3.1g protein / 0.6g salt

COFFEE & PECAN
MINI BREAKFAST MUFFINS

Sometimes you feel you need a sweet hit in the morning to get you through the first few hours. These little muffins provide that with none of the sugar highs and crashes.

MAKES: 9   **PREP TIME:** 25 mins   **COOK TIME:** 20 mins

INGREDIENTS

50 g/1¾ oz coconut flour

¼ tsp baking powder

½ tsp bicarbonate of soda

1 tbsp stevia

30 g/1 oz pecan nuts, roughly chopped

150 ml/5 fl oz soured cream

5 tbsp vegetable oil

2 large eggs, beaten

5 tbsp prepared espresso or strong instant coffee

1 tsp rice malt syrup

sea salt (optional)

1. Preheat the oven to 170°C/325°F/Gas Mark 3. Put nine mini muffin cases into a mini muffin tray.

2. Put the flour, baking powder, bicarbonate of soda, stevia, 20 g/¾ oz pecan nuts and a small pinch of salt, if using, in a large bowl and mix well. Add the soured cream, oil, eggs and 4 tablespoons of espresso, and stir until evenly mixed. Leave to stand for a moment, then spoon the mixture into the mini muffin cases.

3. Bake for 20 minutes, or until well risen and the tops spring back when pressed with a fingertip. Leave to cool for 5 minutes, then transfer to a wire rack.

4. To make the topping, put the rice malt syrup and remaining 1 tablespoon of espresso in a bowl and mix. Spoon a small drizzle over each muffin. Sprinkle on the remaining 10 g/¼ oz pecan nuts and serve warm, or store in an airtight container for up to two days.

TIP: *Baking with rice malt syrup is similar to baking with sugar in terms of quantity and texture. However, be aware that it can burn quickly. You can prevent this by loosely placing a sheet of baking paper over the top of your bake to protect the exposed areas while allowing the rest to bake.*

per muffin: 170 Kcals / 16.6g fat / 3.2g sat fat / 1.6g carbs / 1.1g sugars / 0.5g fibre / 3.6g protein / 0.5g salt

CHIA SEED & PISTACHIO BREAKFAST PUDDING

Overnight soaking in creamy almond milk turns chia seeds into a simple, nutritious and delicious breakfast pudding reminiscent of tapioca. Fresh berries add a burst of flavour and sweetness, while chopped pistachio nuts add a nice crunch.

SERVES: 4   **PREP TIME:** 5 mins   **COOK TIME:** none

INGREDIENTS

225 ml/8 fl oz unsweetened almond milk

225 ml/8 fl oz low-fat natural yogurt

2 tbsp pure maple syrup

1½ tsp vanilla extract

pinch of salt

35 g/1¼ oz chia seeds

225 g/8 oz strawberries, sliced

40 g/1½ oz pistachio nuts, toasted and chopped

maple syrup, for drizzling (optional)

1. Put the almond milk, yogurt, maple syrup, vanilla extract and salt into a medium-sized bowl and stir to combine.

2. Stir in the chia seeds and leave to stand for about 30 minutes at room temperature. Stir the mixture well to make sure the seeds are well incorporated, then cover and chill in the refrigerator for at least 8 hours or overnight.

3. To serve, spoon the pudding into serving bowls and top with the strawberries, nuts and a drizzle of maple syrup, if using.

per serving: 190 Kcals / 8.9g fat / 1.4g sat fat / 21.8g carbs / 13.7g sugars / 5.7g fibre / 6.9g protein / 0.5g salt

PUMPKIN & PECAN PANCAKES

Adding nuts and nutrient-rich pumpkin to these mouth-watering pancakes gives them a real health boost, without losing any of the pancake pleasure.

SERVES: 6   **PREP TIME:** 15 mins   **COOK TIME:** 30 mins

INGREDIENTS

140 g/5 oz plain flour

20 g/¾ oz chopped pecan nuts

50 g/1¾ oz soft light brown sugar

2 tsp baking powder

½ tsp cinnamon

¼ tsp salt

1 egg

300 ml/10 fl oz semi-skimmed buttermilk

200 g/7 oz peeled and cooked pumpkin, (prepared weight), mashed

1 tsp vanilla extract

1 spray vegetable oil spray

125 ml/4 fl oz maple syrup, to serve

1. In a medium bowl, combine the flour, pecan nuts, brown sugar, baking powder, cinnamon and salt. In a large bowl, whisk the egg, buttermilk, pumpkin and vanilla extract. Whisk the dry ingredients into the wet ingredients and mix well.

2. Spray a non-stick frying pan with the vegetable oil spray and heat over a medium–high heat. When hot, ladle in the batter 50 ml/1¾ fl oz at a time to make 8–10-cm/3–4-inch pancakes.

3. Cook for about 2–3 minutes or until bubbles begin to burst in the top and the base is lightly coloured. Flip over and cook for about a further 2 minutes or until the second side is lightly coloured. Serve immediately with maple syrup.

TIP: *Substitute the plain flour with wholemeal flour to increase the fibre content.*

per serving: 228 Kcals / 4.5g fat / 0.8g sat fat / 43.7g carbs / 28g sugars / 0.6g fibre / 6g protein / 0.6g salt

BANANA, GOJI & HAZELNUT BREAD

On mornings when you don't have time to eat breakfast before you leave, wrap a slice of this superfood-packed bread in baking paper and enjoy it when you get to work.

MAKES: 10 slices **PREP TIME:** 20 mins, plus cooling **COOK TIME:** 1 hour

INGREDIENTS

10 g/¼ oz butter, for greasing

85 g/3 oz butter, softened

115 g/4 oz light muscovado sugar

2 eggs

3 bananas (500 g/ 1 lb 2 oz unpeeled weight), peeled and mashed

115 g/4 oz plain wholemeal flour

115 g/4 oz plain white flour

2 tsp baking powder

55 g/2 oz unblanched hazelnuts, roughly chopped

40 g/1½ oz goji berries

40 g/1½ oz dried banana chips

1. Preheat the oven to 180°C/350°F/Gas Mark 4. Grease a 900-g/2-lb loaf tin and line the base and two long sides with baking paper.

2. Cream the butter and sugar together in a large bowl. Beat in the eggs, one at a time, then the bananas.

3. Put the wholemeal flour, white flour and baking powder into a bowl and mix well. Add to the banana mixture and beat until smooth. Add the hazelnuts and goji berries and stir well.

4. Spoon the batter into the prepared tin, smooth the top, then sprinkle with the banana chips. Bake for 50–60 minutes, or until well risen, has cracked slightly, and a skewer inserted into the centre comes out clean.

5. Leave to cool for 5 minutes, then loosen the edges with a round-bladed knife and turn out onto a wire rack. Leave to cool completely, then peel away the paper. Store in an airtight container for up to 3 days.

TIP: *Naturally rich in fruit sugar and starch, bananas are an energy-boosting food. They have plenty of potassium, helping to regulate blood pressure and lower the risk of heart attacks and strokes. They also contain the amino acid tryptophan and vitamin B6, which help in the production of mood-boosting serotonin.*

per slice: 276 Kcals / 10g fat / 2.5g sat fat / 43g carbs / 19g sugars / 3.5g fibre / 5.5g protein / 0.8g salt

LUNCH & DINNER

SPICY PEANUT SOUP

This spicy and satisfying soup gets rich flavour from peanut butter and a kick from herbs and chillies. Serve it with hunks of crusty bread for dunking or over steamed rice.

SERVES: 4   **PREP TIME:** 15 mins   **COOK TIME:** 35—40 mins

INGREDIENTS

1 tbsp vegetable oil

1 small onion, chopped

1 tbsp finely chopped fresh ginger

2 garlic cloves, finely chopped

½ tsp ground cumin

½ tsp pepper

¼ tsp ground cinnamon

¼ tsp cayenne pepper

¼ tsp turmeric

1½ tsp salt

2–4 serrano chillies, chopped

350 g/12 oz sweet potatoes, peeled and diced

750 ml/1¼ pints vegetable stock

400 g/14 oz canned chopped tomatoes, with their can juices

125 g/4½ oz smooth peanut butter

125 ml/4 fl oz coconut milk

juice of 1 lemon

2 tbsp chopped fresh coriander leaves

2 spring onions, thinly sliced, and chopped fresh coriander leaves to garnish

1. Heat the oil in a medium-sized saucepan over a medium heat. Add the onion and cook, stirring frequently, for 10 minutes until soft. Stir in the ginger, garlic, cumin, pepper, cinnamon, cayenne pepper, turmeric and salt.

2. Add the chillies, sweet potatoes and stock and increase the heat to medium–high. Bring the mixture to the boil, then reduce the heat to medium–low and simmer for 20 minutes until the sweet potatoes are tender.

3. Add the tomatoes with their can juices and the peanut butter. Purée the soup in a blender. Return the soup to the pan and stir in the coconut milk, lemon juice and coriander. Heat over a medium heat until heated through. Serve hot, garnished with the spring onions and chopped coriander, if using.

per serving: 402 Kcals / 26.6g fat / 9.2g sat fat / 34.9g carbs / 13.3g sugars / 5.8g fibre / 11.7g protein / 4.5g salt

1

2

3

CARROT & ALMOND SOUP

This smooth and comforting soup is a classic pairing combining the antioxidant power of carrots with the vitamin-busting benefits of the almond. Ultimately, though, this is a delicious soup that will suit even the fussiest of palates.

SERVES: 4   **PREP TIME:** 15 mins   **COOK TIME:** 30 mins

INGREDIENTS

2 tbsp olive oil

1 yellow onion, diced

2 garlic cloves, very finely chopped

450 g/1 lb carrots, sliced

1 tsp salt

1½ tsp ground cumin

½ tsp ground coriander

½ tsp pepper

½ tsp cayenne pepper

1 tsp sweet paprika

¼ tsp ground ginger

1.5 litres/2½ pints chicken stock

35 g/1¼ oz blanched almonds

225 g/8 oz Spanish chorizo, diced

55 g/2 oz flaked almonds

juice of 1 lemon

15 g/½ oz fresh coriander leaves, roughly chopped

1. Put the oil into a large saucepan and heat over a medium–high heat. Add the onion and garlic and cook for 5 minutes, stirring frequently, until the onion is soft. Add the carrots, salt, cumin, ground coriander, pepper, cayenne pepper, paprika and ginger and cook, stirring, for a further minute. Add the stock and blanched almonds and bring to the boil. Reduce the heat to low and simmer, uncovered, for about 20 minutes, until the carrots are very soft.

2. Meanwhile, heat a heavy frying pan over a medium–high heat. Add the chorizo and cook for 6–8 minutes, stirring frequently, until the fat begins to render and the meat begins to brown. Add the flaked almonds and continue to cook, stirring frequently, until the meat is brown and the almonds are golden and crisp. Transfer to a plate lined with kitchen paper to drain.

3. Purée the soup with a hand-held blender until smooth. Bring to a simmer over a medium heat, then stir in the lemon juice and fresh coriander.

4. Serve the soup hot, garnished with the crispy chorizo and flaked almonds.

per serving: 492 Kcals / 42.4g fat / 11g sat fat / 12.7g carbs / 3g sugars / 3.4g fibre / 19.6g protein / 6.8g salt

CURRIED CHICKEN SALAD WRAPS

This chicken salad is dressed up with spicy curry powder, creamy mayonnaise, sweet raisins and crunchy pecan nuts. Wrapped in flour tortillas, it makes a delicious and filling lunch.

SERVES: 4   **PREP TIME:** 5–8 mins   **COOK TIME:** 10 mins

INGREDIENTS

4 flour tortillas

350 g/12 oz cooked chicken, diced or shredded

90 ml/3 fl oz mayonnaise

1 tsp Dijon mustard

½ tsp salt

2 tbsp curry powder

50 g/1¾ oz raisins

40 g/1½ oz unsalted, toasted cashew nuts, roughly chopped

4 large lettuce leaves

1. Preheat the oven to 200°C/400°F/Gas Mark 6.

2. Wrap the tortillas in foil and heat in the preheated oven for about 10 minutes.

3. Meanwhile, put the chicken, mayonnaise, mustard, salt, curry powder, raisins and nuts into a medium-sized bowl and stir until well combined.

4. Divide the chicken mixture between the warmed tortillas, add a lettuce leaf to each and roll up, folding up the ends of the tortillas to hold in the filling. Serve immediately.

TIP: *This is a great way to use up leftover roast chicken, turning a delicious Sunday dinner into an enviably tasty weekday lunch.*

per serving: 489 Kcals / 21.2g fat / 4.6g sat fat / 43.8g carbs / 11.9g sugars / 3.5g fibre / 31.7g protein / 1.8g salt

SPINACH, PEAR & WALNUT SALAD

Spinach is a veritable nutritional powerhouse – it has long been associated with energy renewal and its rich iron content improves the quality of red blood cells. Combining it with ripe pears, walnuts and soft blue cheese creates a real treat of a salad.

SERVES: 2   **PREP TIME:** 25 mins   **COOK TIME:** none

INGREDIENTS

DRESSING

1 tbsp extra virgin olive oil

2 tbsp balsamic vinegar

salt and pepper (optional)

SALAD

100 g/3½ oz baby leaf spinach

2 ripe pears, quartered, cored and thinly sliced

25 g/1 oz walnuts, chopped

85 g/3 oz soft blue cheese, crumbled, to serve

1. Put the oil and vinegar into a small bowl. Season to taste with salt and pepper, if using, and whisk until thoroughly combined.

2. Put the spinach leaves into a salad bowl and add just enough of the dressing to lightly coat the leaves. Add the pears and the walnuts and toss to combine. Add the remaining dressing, to taste. Serve with the cheese scattered on top.

per serving: 419 Kcals / 27.5g fat / 9.7g sat fat / 34.3g carbs / 20.4g sugars / 7.4g fibre / 13.2g protein / 1.3g salt

RED CABBAGE WITH NUTS, MUSHROOMS & BACON

Hazelnuts have significant health benefits – they are rich in dietary fibre, vitamins and minerals and are packed with phyto-chemicals which offer multiple health-giving properties. They also have a pleasant sweet taste when served in a salad such as this one.

SERVES: 4   **PREP TIME:** 10 mins   **COOK TIME:** 35 mins

INGREDIENTS

½ head of red cabbage

2 tbsp rapeseed oil

6 thin bacon rashers, chopped

1 onion, chopped

2 tsp thyme leaves

150 g/5½ oz chestnut mushrooms, roughly chopped

55 g/2 oz toasted hazelnuts, chopped

grated zest of 1 lemon

1 tsp sea salt flakes

½ tsp pepper

½ tsp sugar

2 tbsp cider vinegar

225 ml/8 fl oz beef stock

15 g/½ oz fresh parsley, chopped

lightly salted butter, to serve

1. Cut the cabbage in quarters lengthways, discarding the tough central core. Slice the leaves widthways into ribbons.

2. Heat the oil in a flameproof casserole dish over a medium–high heat. Add the bacon and cook for about 5 minutes until crisp.

3. Reduce the heat to medium, add the onion and thyme and cook for 5 minutes, until the onion is translucent. Add the mushrooms and cabbage and cook for a further 5 minutes, until starting to soften.

4. Stir in the nuts, lemon zest, salt, pepper and sugar, and cook for a further 3 minutes. Pour in the vinegar and stock, cover and bring to the boil, then reduce the heat and simmer for 15 minutes until the cabbage is tender.

5. Transfer to a warmed serving dish. Stir in the parsley and a little butter and serve immediately.

per serving: 386 Kcals / 32.4g fat / 10g sat fat / 15.6g carbs / 7g sugars / 4.5g fibre / 12.3g protein / 3.4 salt

HAM & BRIE SANDWICHES WITH PISTACHIO TAPENADE

The advantage of this pistachio tapenade is that once the figs are soft, you can just whizz the ingredients up and it is ready. The tapenade can be combined with raw vegetables as a dip, mixed with penne pesto pasta, or used cold as a sandwich spread, as here.

SERVES: 4   **PREP TIME:** 10 mins   **COOK TIME:** 30 mins

INGREDIENTS

TAPENADE

90 g/3¼ oz dried figs, quartered

50 g/1¾ oz stoned kalamata olives

60 g/2¼ oz roasted, unsalted pistachio nuts

juice and grated zest of 1 lemon

2 tsp capers, drained

½ tsp pepper

SANDWICHES

1 baguette, cut into 4 pieces and slit

115 g/4 oz Brie, chilled and sliced

8 thin slices of Parma ham

1. To make the tapenade, place the figs in a small saucepan and add water to just cover them. Bring to the boil over a medium–high heat, reduce the heat to low, and simmer for 20–30 minutes until the figs are very soft and most of the water has evaporated.

2. Transfer the figs, along with any remaining liquid, to a food processor. Add the olives, pistachio nuts, lemon zest and juice, capers and pepper and pulse to a chunky purée.

3. To make the sandwiches, spread one side of each baguette piece with about 2 tablespoons of tapenade. Divide the cheese evenly between the sandwiches. Top the cheese on each sandwich with two slices of ham. Close up the sandwiches and serve at room temperature.

per serving: 458 Kcals / 21g fat / 7.5g sat fat / 47.5g carbs / 12.4g sugars / 5.4g fibre / 22.5g protein / 2.6g salt

WARM QUINOA, ROAST PUMPKIN & PINE NUT SALAD

Quinoa has long been prized for its flavour and ability to keep you feeling full. Loaded with protein and vitamins, it is an ideal choice for a salad.

SERVES: 2   **PREP TIME:** 20 mins   **COOK TIME:** 30 mins

INGREDIENTS

100 g/3½ oz white quinoa, rinsed

350 ml/12 fl oz cold water

200 g/7 oz pumpkin flesh, cut into bite-sized chunks

4 tbsp olive oil

pinch of cayenne pepper

pinch of salt

20 g/¾ oz pine nuts

25 g/1 oz fresh flat-leaf parsley, roughly chopped

20 g/¾ oz baby spinach

juice of ¼ lemon

salt and pepper (optional)

1. Preheat the oven to 180°C/350°F/Gas Mark 4. Put the quinoa in a saucepan. Add the water, bring to the boil, then cover and simmer over a very low heat for 10 minutes. Remove from the heat, but leave the pan covered for a further 7 minutes to allow the grains to swell. Fluff up with a fork.

2. Meanwhile, put the pumpkin and 2 tablespoons of the oil in a large roasting tin, sprinkle with the cayenne pepper and salt and toss well. Roast in the preheated oven for 25 minutes, or until crisp on the edges and tender. Tip into a large bowl.

3. Toast the pine nuts in a dry frying pan over a high heat until they are light brown, then tip them into the bowl. Gently mix in the quinoa, parsley and spinach, taking care that nothing breaks up, then season with salt and pepper, if using.

4. Divide the salad between two plates, drizzle with the remaining oil and the lemon juice.

ALMOND MILK

Almond milk is a healthy alternative to cow's milk and there are many reasons for this. For one thing, it's low in fat and calories. It is also a great source of the antioxidant vitamin E, which helps to prevent cancer and premature ageing and helps keep your skin glowing, and of many other vitamins and minerals, such as copper, zinc, iron, magnesium, manganese, calcium, phosphorus, potassium and selenium. Flavonoids in almond milk also help fight free radicals in the body, thereby protecting you from various degenerative diseases such as osteoporosis and type 2 diabetes. Almond milk is free of both cholesterol and saturated fat and is high in omega-3 fatty acids, which help lower cholesterol and protect the heart.

You can use almond milk in the same way that you'd use cow's milk: Put it in your coffee or tea, pour it over cereal, use it as a substitute for cow's milk in recipes, or drink it straight out of a glass.

Almond milk is easy to make at home – and making your own is considerably less expensive than buying it. Better still, while ready-made almond milk is often loaded with sweeteners, preservatives, thickeners and other additives, home-made almond milk is made with nothing but raw almonds and water. This plain version is delicious on its own and is perfect for using in our recipes instead of buying ready-made almond milk, but you can also add natural sweeteners (honey, sugar, maple syrup, agave syrup or stevia) or spices (cinnamon or vanilla extract) to turn it into a sweet treat in its own right.

2

3

HOW TO MAKE ALMOND MILK

INGREDIENTS

140 g/5 oz raw almonds

475 ml/16 fl oz water, plus extra for soaking

1. Place the almonds in a medium-sized bowl and cover with 2.5 cm/1 inch of water. Soak overnight and then drain, discarding the soaking water.

2. Place the almonds in a blender with the water and process until the nuts are pulverized.

3. Strain the mixture through muslin into a jug or jar, squeezing out as much liquid as you can. Discard the solids. The almond milk can be used right away or stored in a covered container in the refrigerator for up to a week.

CHICKEN & PEANUT CURRY

If you like warmth and an element of spice in your meals then here is a dish offering the magical combination of chicken, peanuts and spices.

SERVES: 4   **PREP TIME:** 15 mins   **COOK TIME:** 20 mins

INGREDIENTS

75 g/2¾ oz roasted, unsalted peanuts

4 chicken breast fillets

1 tbsp vegetable oil

1 shallot, diced

2–4 tbsp Thai red curry paste

400 ml/14 fl oz canned coconut milk

1 tbsp Thai fish sauce

1 tbsp soft light brown sugar

juice of 1 lime

25 g/1 oz chopped fresh coriander leaves

chopped fresh coriander, to garnish (optional)

750 g/1 lb 10 oz long grain brown rice, cooked, to serve

1. Put the peanuts into a food processor and process for 2–3 minutes until they form a smooth butter.

2. Line a large steamer basket with baking paper and place the chicken fillets on the paper. Place the steamer over boiling water, cover and steam for 10–12 minutes, until the chicken is tender and cooked through. Cut into the middle to check that the meat is no longer pink. Any juices that run out should be clear and piping hot with visible steam rising.

3. Meanwhile, heat the oil in a large frying pan and add the shallot. Cook, stirring frequently, for 5 minutes, or until soft. Add the curry paste and cook, stirring, for a further minute.

4. Open the can of coconut milk and scoop off the thick cream that has risen to the top. Add the cream to the pan and cook, stirring, until it begins to bubble. Add the remaining coconut milk along with the peanut butter, Thai fish sauce and sugar. Bring to the boil, then reduce the heat to low. Simmer for 5 minutes, or until the sauce thickens.

5. Stir in the lime juice and coriander. Serve the chicken fillets topped with a generous amount of the sauce and garnished with chopped coriander, if using.

per serving: 795 Kcals / 41.4g fat / 22.2g sat fat / 62g carbs / 8.5g sugars / 5.7g fibre / 46.2g protein / 1.6g salt

MACADAMIA-CRUSTED SALMON WITH PINEAPPLE SALSA

The tropical flavours of macadamia nuts, coconut and pineapple make this simple salmon dish extra special, and it's also a refreshingly easy dish to prepare.

SERVES: 4   PREP TIME: 20 mins, plus resting   COOK TIME: 10–15 mins

INGREDIENTS

1 tbsp vegetable oil, for brushing

150 g/5½ oz chopped, roasted, unsalted macadamia nuts

50 g/1¾ oz panko breadcrumbs

2 tbsp plain flour

55 g/2 oz unsalted butter, melted

4 salmon fillets, 175 g/6 oz each

1 tsp salt

½ tsp pepper

2 tbsp coconut milk

SALSA

325 g/11½ oz chopped pineapple

½ red onion, diced

2 jalapeño chillies, deseeded and finely chopped

10 g/¼ oz fresh coriander, finely chopped

½ tsp salt

juice of 1 lime

1 tbsp olive oil

1. Preheat the oven to 220°C/425°F/Gas Mark 7 and line a baking sheet with baking paper. Brush the paper with the oil.

2. Put the nuts, breadcrumbs, flour and butter into a medium-sized bowl and stir to mix well.

3. Season the salmon fillets on both sides with the salt and pepper and place them on the prepared baking sheet. Brush the tops of the fillets with the coconut milk. Top each fillet with a quarter of the nut and breadcrumb mixture, pressing it into the fish in an even layer.

4. Bake the fish in the preheated oven for 10–15 minutes, or until the topping is golden brown and the fish is cooked and flakes easily with a fork.

5. Meanwhile, make the salsa. Put all of the ingredients into a bowl and stir together until well combined.

6. Remove the fish from the oven and leave to rest for a few minutes. Serve hot, topped with the pineapple salsa.

per serving: 927 Kcals / 72g fat / 19.1g sat fat / 34.5g carbs / 11.9g sugars / 8.5g fibre / 38.4g protein / 1.6g salt

2

3

5

PISTACHIO-CRUSTED LAMB CHOPS

*Chopped pistachios and garlic make a tasty, crunchy coating for meaty lamb chops.
A sauce of sweet dried cherries and ruby port makes this an elegant dinner party dish.
Serve the chops on a bed of creamy polenta for an extra special touch.*

SERVES: 4   **PREP TIME:** 20 mins, plus resting   **COOK TIME:** 40 mins

INGREDIENTS

2 tbsp olive oil

½ onion, thinly sliced

225 ml/8 fl oz ruby port

140 g/5 oz dried sweet
cherries, roughly chopped

225 ml/8 fl oz chicken stock

1 tbsp clear honey

1¾ tsp salt

3 garlic cloves

100 g/3½ oz roasted,
unsalted pistachio nuts

8 lamb chops

½ tsp pepper

1 tbsp Dijon mustard mixed
with 1 tbsp water

1. Preheat the oven to 220°C/425°F/Gas Mark 7.

2. Heat the oil in a heavy frying pan over a medium-high heat. Add the onion and cook for about 5 minutes, stirring occasionally, until soft. Add the port, cherries, stock, honey and ¾ teaspoon of the salt and bring just to the boil. Reduce the heat to medium-low and simmer for about 20 minutes until the sauce is thick and syrupy.

3. Meanwhile, put the garlic into the food processor and pulse until finely chopped. Add the nuts and pulse until finely chopped. Transfer to a plate.

4. Season the lamb chops on all sides with the remaining salt and the pepper, then brush with the mustard mixture. Press each lamb chop into the nut mixture to coat well all over.

5. Transfer the chops to a baking tray and bake in the preheated oven for 6 minutes. Turn over and cook for a further 6 minutes for medium rare, or 7–8 minutes for well done. Remove from the oven and loosely tent with foil. Leave to rest for 5 minutes before serving.

6. Serve hot, with the sauce spooned over the top.

per serving: 859 Kcals / 47.1g fat / 16.2g sat fat / 50g carbs / 29.4g sugars / 11.7g fibre / 43.4g protein / 3.5g salt

NUT ROAST

The benefit of a nut roast is that you can make it in advance, reducing the preparation if you are planning to serve it with all the standard roast trimmings. The dish can also be served cold with a crispy salad, in sandwiches or with a warming bowl of soup.

SERVES: 6   **PREP TIME:** 20 mins   **COOK TIME:** 35–40 mins

INGREDIENTS

1 tbsp olive oil, for brushing

2 tbsp olive oil

1 large onion, finely chopped

100 g/3½ oz ground almonds

100 g/3½ oz cashew nuts, finely chopped

55 g/2 oz fresh wholemeal breadcrumbs

100 ml/3½ fl oz vegetable stock

finely grated rind and juice of 1 small lemon

1 tbsp finely chopped rosemary leaves

salt and pepper (optional)

fresh rosemary sprigs and lemon slices, to garnish (optional)

1. Preheat the oven to 200°C/400°F/Gas Mark 6. Brush a 750-ml/1¼-pint loaf tin with oil and line with baking paper.

2. Heat the oil in a large saucepan, add the onion and fry over a medium heat, stirring, for 3–4 minutes until soft.

3. Stir in the almonds, cashew nuts, breadcrumbs, stock, lemon rind and juice and rosemary. Season with salt and pepper, if using, and stir well to mix.

4. Press the mixture into the prepared tin, brush with oil and bake in the preheated oven for 30–35 minutes until golden brown and firm.

5. Turn out and serve hot, garnished with rosemary sprigs, lemon slices and pepper, if using.

per serving: 429 Kcals / 34.8g fat / 4.5g sat fat / 22.3g carbs / 5.4g sugars / 12.2g fibre / 0.3g protein / 5g salt

CHICKPEA
WALNUT PATTIES

These hearty patties are very similar to falafel, but have the added richness and flavour of walnuts. They are delicious served on toasted hamburger buns with lettuce, tomato and mayonnaise or tahini sauce.

SERVES: 4   **PREP TIME:** 15 mins, plus chilling   **COOK TIME:** 10 mins

INGREDIENTS

2 garlic cloves

1 shallot

425 g/15 oz canned chickpeas, drained and rinsed

15 g/½ oz fresh flat-leaf parsley

1 tsp ground coriander

1 tsp ground cumin

½ tsp salt

⅛ tsp cayenne pepper

2 tbsp olive oil

2 tbsp plain flour

½ tsp baking powder

60 g/2¼ oz roasted, unsalted walnuts, roughly chopped

2 tbsp sunflower oil, for frying

1. Put the garlic and shallot into a food processor and pulse to chop. Add the chickpeas, parsley, coriander, cumin, salt, cayenne pepper, olive oil and flour and pulse to a chunky purée. Add the baking powder and pulse once to incorporate. Add the walnuts and pulse once to incorporate.

2. Shape the chickpea mixture into four equal-sized patties, about 10 cm/4 inches in diameter. Chill in the refrigerator for at least 30 minutes or overnight.

3. Heat the sunflower oil in a large frying pan over a medium–high heat. Add the patties and cook for 4–5 minutes on each side until golden brown. Serve hot.

per serving: 320 Kcals / 24.7g fat / 2.6g sat fat / 18.1g carbs / 3.5g sugars / 5.2g fibre / 7g protein / 0.9g salt

1

3

5

PUMPKIN & CHESTNUT RISOTTO

This comforting dish is full of nutritious content – pumpkin has vital antioxidants and vitamins, and chestnuts offer minerals, vitamins and phytonutrients.

SERVES: 4   **PREP TIME:** 20 mins   **COOK TIME:** 1 hour

INGREDIENTS

1 tbsp olive oil

40 g/1½ oz butter

1 small onion, finely chopped

225 g/8 oz pumpkin, diced

225 g/8 oz chestnuts, cooked and shelled

280 g/10 oz risotto rice

150 ml/5 fl oz dry white wine

1 tsp crumbled saffron threads, dissolved in 4 tbsp of the stock

1 litre/1¾ pints simmering vegetable stock

salt and pepper (optional)

85 g/3 oz freshly grated Parmesan cheese

freshly grated Parmesan cheese, to serve (optional)

1. Heat the oil with 25 g/1 oz of the butter in a deep saucepan over a medium heat until the butter has melted. Stir in the onion and pumpkin and cook, stirring occasionally, for 5 minutes, or until the onion is soft and starting to turn golden and the pumpkin begins to colour.

2. Roughly chop the chestnuts and add to the mixture. Stir thoroughly to coat.

3. Reduce the heat, add the rice and mix to coat in oil and butter. Cook, stirring constantly, for 2–3 minutes, or until the grains are translucent. Add the wine and cook, stirring constantly, for 1 minute, until it has reduced.

4. Add the saffron liquid to the rice and cook, stirring constantly, until all the liquid has been completely absorbed.

5. Gradually add the simmering stock, a ladleful at a time, stirring constantly. Add more liquid as the rice absorbs each addition. Increase the heat to medium so that the liquid bubbles. Cook for 20 minutes, or until all the liquid has been absorbed and the rice is creamy. Season with salt and pepper, if using.

6. Remove the risotto from the heat and add the remaining butter. Mix well, then stir in the cheese until it melts. Adjust the seasoning, if necessary. Spoon the risotto onto four warmed plates and serve immediately, sprinkled with grated cheese, if using.

per serving: 602 Kcals / 20g fat / 10g sat fat / 81g carbs / 8g sugars / 5.4g fibre / 15.5g protein / 2.1g salt

TAGLIATELLE WITH HAZELNUT PESTO

Fresh and light and simple as you like, this protein-packed vegetarian main dish served with a hazelnut pesto can be made in a matter of minutes.

SERVES: 4　　**PREP TIME:** 5 mins　　**COOK TIME:** 10–12 mins

INGREDIENTS

1 tsp salt

350 g/12 oz dried tagliatelle

175 g/6 oz fresh or frozen broad beans

PESTO

1 garlic clove, roughly chopped

55 g/2 oz hazelnuts

100 g/3½ oz wild rocket

4 tbsp olive oil

salt and pepper (optional)

1. To make the pesto, place the garlic, hazelnuts, rocket and oil in a food processor and process to a rough paste. Season to taste with salt and pepper, if using.

2. Add 1 teaspoon of salt to a large pan of water and bring to the boil. Add the pasta, return to the boil and cook for 8–10 minutes, or until tender but still firm to the bite. Add the beans 3–4 minutes before the end of the cooking time.

3. Drain the pasta and beans well, then tip back into the pan. Add the pesto and toss to coat evenly. Serve immediately.

per serving: 522 Kcals / 22g fat / 2.5g sat fat / 71g carbs / 3g sugars / 9g fibre / 15g protein / 0.1g salt

1

2

3

BAKING & DESSERTS

CHOCOLATE-DIPPED CHERRY & PISTACHIO BISCOTTI

These crunchy biscotti, studded with green nuts and red cherries and draped in dark chocolate, make a festive addition to a cookie platter or a lovely Christmas gift.

MAKES: 40   PREP TIME: 25 mins, plus cooling   COOK TIME: 45 mins

INGREDIENTS

2 sprays non-stick cooking spray

250 g/9 oz plain flour

125 g/4½ oz wholemeal flour

¼ tsp salt

200 g/7 oz granulated sugar

3 eggs

2 tbsp vegetable oil

1 tbsp vanilla extract

40 g/1½ oz dried cherries, roughly chopped

60 g/2¼ oz roasted, unsalted pistachio nuts

10 g/¼ oz flour, for dusting

280 g/10 oz plain chocolate, chopped

1. Preheat the oven to 180°C/350°F/Gas Mark 4 and line a large baking sheet with baking paper. Spray the paper with cooking spray.

2. Put both flours and salt into a mixing bowl. Put the sugar and eggs into a separate mixing bowl and beat with a hand-held electric mixer on high speed for 3–4 minutes, until the mixture is thick and pale yellow. Add the oil and vanilla extract and beat until incorporated. Add the dry mixture to the wet, and beat until combined. Add the cherries and nuts.

3. Divide the dough into two equal-sized pieces and turn them onto the baking sheet. With floured hands, shape each piece of dough into a 25-cm/10-inch loaf and flatten it to 2.5 cm/1 inch, squaring off the edges with your hands.

4. Bake in the preheated oven for 25 minutes, or until light brown. Remove from the oven and leave to cool on the baking sheet for about 10 minutes. Meanwhile, reduce the oven temperature to 160°C/325°F/Gas Mark 3.

5. Slice each loaf into 20 x 1-cm/½-inch thick slices. Arrange cut side down on the baking sheet and return to the oven for 10 minutes. Turn the slices and bake for 10 more minutes. Remove from the oven, and cool on a wire rack.

6. Put the chocolate into a heatproof bowl over a saucepan of gently simmering water and heat until melted. Dip one flat side of the biscotti into the melted chocolate, then return to the lined baking sheet, setting the biscotti on the uncoated side, and leave to cool for 10–15 minutes until the chocolate is set. Serve at room temperature.

per biscotti: 120 Kcals / 4.8g fat / 2g sat fat / 16.7g carbs / 7.3g sugars / 1.7g fibre / 2.4g protein / trace salt

CHOCOLATE & ALMOND MINI CAKES

These delightful mini cakes have nuts both inside and out, with ground almonds mixed in the cake base and a sumptuous topping of butter, soft brown sugar and flaked almonds.

MAKES: 12 **PREP TIME:** 15 mins **COOK TIME:** 22–24 mins

INGREDIENTS

MINI CAKES

70 g/2½ oz ground almonds

60 g/2¼ oz plain flour

40 g/1½ oz cocoa powder

1 tsp baking powder

¼ tsp salt

50 g/1¾ oz unsalted butter, at room temperature

60 g/2¼ oz caster sugar

2 tsp vanilla extract

2 eggs

60 ml/2 fl oz double cream

TOPPING

55 g/2 oz flaked almonds

1 tbsp soft light brown sugar

1 tbsp unsalted butter, melted

1. Preheat the oven to 180°C/350°F/Gas Mark 4 and line a 12-hole bun tin with paper cases.

2. Put the ground almonds, flour, cocoa powder, baking powder and salt into a medium-sized bowl and stir to combine.

3. Put the butter and sugar into a large bowl and cream with a hand-held electric mixer until light and fluffy. Add the vanilla extract and the eggs, one at a time, and beat on a medium–high speed until combined. Add half of the flour mixture and beat on medium–high until incorporated. Scrape down the side of the bowl, add the cream and beat to incorporate. Scrape down the side of the bowl again, add the remaining flour mixture and beat on medium-high until incorporated.

4. Scoop the batter into the prepared tin, filling each paper case about half full.

5. To make the topping, put the almonds and sugar into a small bowl and stir to combine. Add the butter and mix well to combine.

6. Divide the topping mixture between the paper cases. Bake in the preheated oven for 22–24 minutes, or until a cocktail stick inserted into the centre of a cake comes out clean. Remove from the oven and leave to cool in the tin for 1–2 minutes, then transfer to a wire rack and leave to cool completely. Serve at room temperature.

per cake: 181 Kcals / 13g fat / 4.8g sat fat / 14.3g carbs / 6.9g sugars / 2.3g fibre / 4.6g protein / 0.3g salt

SUPERFOOD CHOCOLATE BARK

The darker the chocolate, the less sugar and more cocoa butter it contains,
so always choose chocolate with at least 70% cocoa solids.

SERVES: 6   **PREP TIME:** 20 mins   **COOK TIME:** 5 mins

INGREDIENTS

100 g/3½ oz plain
chocolate, 70% cocoa
solids, broken into pieces

85 g/3 oz mixed
Brazil nuts, unblanched
almonds and pistachio nuts,
roughly chopped

2 tbsp dried goji berries,
roughly chopped

2 tbsp dried cranberries,
roughly chopped

1 tbsp chia seeds

1. Place the chocolate in a bowl set over a saucepan of gently simmering water and heat for 5 minutes, until the chocolate is melted, making sure that the base of the bowl is not touching the water.

2. Line a large baking sheet with non-stick baking paper. Stir the chocolate, then pour it onto the paper and spread to a 20 x 30-cm/8 x 12-inch rectangle.

3. Sprinkle the nuts, berries and chia seeds over the top, then leave to set in a cool place or the refrigerator.

4. To serve, lift the chocolate off the paper and break into rough-shaped shards. Store in a plastic container in the refrigerator for up to 3 days.

per serving: 227 Kcals / 15.7g fat / 5.3g sat fat / 17.7g carbs / 10.2g sugars / 5.1g fibre / 5.1g protein / trace salt

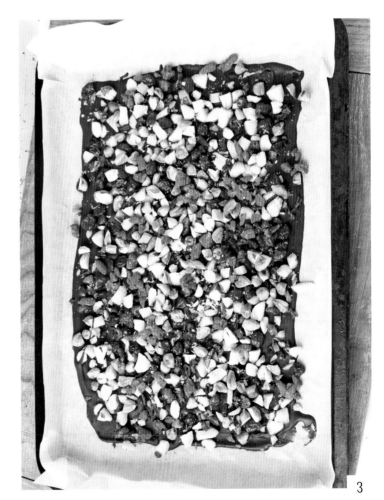

BANANA & MACADAMIA NUT BREAD

Macadamia nuts bring a tropical twist to this banana bread. Served warm on its own or with a little butter, it makes a comforting snack or a hearty breakfast.

MAKES: 10 slices   **PREP TIME:** 15 mins   **COOK TIME:** 1 hour 5 mins

INGREDIENTS

10 g/¼ oz butter, for greasing

125 g/4½ oz plain flour

60 g/2¼ oz wholemeal flour

1 tsp bicarbonate of soda

pinch of salt

2–3 large ripe bananas

100 g/3½ oz granulated sugar

110 g/3¾ oz soft light brown sugar

125 ml/4 fl oz sunflower oil

2 eggs, beaten

1 tsp vanilla extract

75 g/2¾ oz macadamia nuts, roughly chopped

1. Preheat the oven to 180°C/350°F/Gas Mark 4 and grease a 10 x 20-cm/4 x 8-inch loaf tin and line with baking paper.

2. Put the plain flour, wholemeal flour, bicarbonate of soda and salt into a mixing bowl and stir well.

3. Put the bananas into a separate large mixing bowl and mash until smooth. Add the granulated sugar, brown sugar and oil and beat with a hand-held electric mixer until combined. Add the eggs and vanilla extract and beat for 1 minute on medium speed until well combined. Stir in the nuts.

4. Add the flour mixture and stir to combine. Transfer the batter to the prepared tin and bake in the preheated oven for 55 minutes–1 hour 5 minutes, until the outside is brown and a skewer inserted into the centre of the loaf comes out clean.

5. Remove from the oven, transfer to a wire rack in the tin and leave to cool completely. Remove from the tin, cut into slices and serve.

per slice: 364 Kcals / 20.3g fat / 3.1g sat fat / 43.6g carbs / 25.3g sugars / 2.5g fibre / 4.3g protein / 0.5g salt

GINGER, NUT & OAT BISCUITS

Biscuits warm from the oven make a great welcome for children back from school or for guests. Keep the dough in the refrigerator and slice off biscuits, then bake for 15 minutes.

MAKES: 18   **PREP TIME:** 30 mins, plus chilling   **COOK TIME:** 12–15 mins

INGREDIENTS

175 g/6 oz unsalted butter, softened and diced

115 g/4 oz dark muscovado sugar

2.5-cm/1-inch piece fresh ginger, peeled and finely chopped

150 g/5½ oz wholemeal plain flour

85 g/3 oz porridge oats

70 g/2½ oz unblanched hazelnuts, roughly chopped

70 g/2½ oz unblanched almonds, roughly chopped

10 g/¼ oz unsalted butter, for greasing

1. Place a sheet of baking paper about 30 cm/12 inches long on a work surface.

2. Cream the butter, sugar and ginger together in a large bowl. Gradually beat in the flour, then the oats and nuts, until you have a soft dough. Spoon the mixture into a 25-cm/10-inch line along the baking paper, then press it into a 5-cm/2-inch diameter roll. Wrap in the paper and chill in the refrigerator for 30 minutes, or up to three days.

3. Preheat the oven to 180°C/350°F/Gas Mark 4. Grease two baking sheets with butter. Unwrap the biscuit dough and slice off as many biscuits as you require. Arrange on the baking sheets, leaving a little space between each biscuit. Bake for 12–15 minutes, or until cracked and browned at the edges.

4. Leave the biscuits to cool for 5 minutes, then loosen and transfer them to a wire rack to cool completely.

per biscuit: 186 Kcals / 12.7g fat / 5.4g sat fat / 16.6g carbs / 6.8g sugars / 2.2g fibre / 2.3g protein / trace salt

CHOCOLATE & MACADAMIA 'CUPOOKIES'

These delicious mouthfuls are a hybrid between a cupcake and a cookie, and make a nutty and moreish wholesome treat.

MAKES: 12   **PREP TIME:** 30 mins   **COOK TIME:** 20 mins, plus cooling

INGREDIENTS

85 g/3 oz butter, at room temperature

85 g/3 oz crunchy peanut butter

85 g/3 oz light muscovado sugar

2 eggs, beaten

115 g/4 oz wholemeal flour

1 tsp baking powder

55 g/2 oz macadamia nuts, roughly chopped

12 whole macadamia nuts, to decorate

CHOCOLATE FROSTING

100 g/3½ oz plain chocolate, 70% cocoa solids, broken into pieces

25 g/1 oz butter, diced

25 g/1 oz light muscovado sugar

4 tbsp milk

1. Preheat the oven to 180°C/350°F/Gas Mark 4. Line a 12-hole muffin tin with paper cases.

2. Add the butter, peanut butter and sugar to a large bowl or food processor and beat together until light and fluffy.

3. Gradually beat a little of the egg into the butter mixture, alternating with a few spoonfuls of the flour, then continue until all the egg and flour have been added and the mixture is smooth. Beat in the baking powder and chopped nuts.

4. Divide the mixture between the paper cases, bake in the preheated oven for 15 minutes, until risen, golden brown and the tops spring back when lightly pressed with a fingertip. Leave to cool in the tins for 10 minutes.

5. To make the frosting, put the chocolate, butter, sugar and milk into a bowl set over a saucepan of gently simmering water and heat, stirring occasionally, for about 5 minutes, until smooth.

6. Spoon the frosting over the cakes to cover them completely, then top each with a macadamia nut. Leave in a cool place for 30 minutes to cool completely. Remove from the tin and serve, or store any leftovers in a plastic container in the refrigerator for up to 1 day.

per cookie: 274 Kcals / 19.2g fat / 8.3g sat fat / 22.3g carbs / 12.3g sugars / 2.9g fibre / 5.4g protein / 0.2g salt

2

4

5

CHOPPING, GRINDING & TOASTING

CHOPPING NUTS

If you need to chop small quantities of nuts, the best method is the simplest: a knife and a bit of elbow grease. Place the nuts on a chopping board. Hold the knife handle firmly with your dominant hand, and grasp the tip of the blade with your other hand. Rock the knife back and forth across the nuts until you've achieved the desired size. If you are chopping larger quantities of nuts, pulsing them in a food processor works best.

GRINDING NUTS

When grinding nuts for baking recipes, there is always a danger of turning your nuts to butter, but there are a few tricks you can use to prevent this happening. First, make sure that all of your food processor's parts – the bowl and blade especially – are completely dry and cool. The nuts themselves should be at room temperature. Place the nuts in the food processor and pulse, scraping down the side of the bowl every now and then, until you achieve the desired consistency.

TOASTING NUTS

When cooking with nuts, toasting them first may seem redundant, but we think it's well worth the effort. Toasting nuts brings out their deep, earthy flavour and sweetness. It also gives them added crunch.

It is better to toast only the nuts you need as they do lose some of their flavour, but it is possible to store any extra toasted nuts in a sealed container in the refrigerator for 1 to 2 weeks.

IN THE OVEN

The oven method works well for large batches of nuts. Preheat the oven to 180°C/350°F/Gas Mark 4 and spread the nuts on a large baking tray in a single layer. Bake the nuts, shaking the pan once in a while, until they are light golden brown and glossy (this will take anywhere from 5 minutes for small nuts like pine nuts, to 10 minutes for whole almonds or pecans to 25 minutes for shelled peanuts or chestnuts), checking frequently as they will burn easily. Because ovens heat differently, timings are likely to vary.

ON THE HOB

The hob method works well for small batches of nuts. Heat a large frying pan over a medium–high heat. Add the nuts in a single layer. Cook, stirring frequently, until you begin to smell a toasty, nutty aroma and the nuts are light golden-brown (this will take anywhere from 5 minutes for small nuts like pine nuts, to 10 minutes for whole almonds or pecans to 25 minutes for shelled peanuts or chestnuts). Transfer the nuts from the hot pan to a plate or bowl as soon as they reach the toasted stage because they can burn quickly.

IN THE MICROWAVE

The microwave is a great solution when you are pressed for time, although the nuts will not become as beautifully browned as they will if you use either the hob or oven methods. To toast nuts in the microwave, spread them in a single layer in a microwave-safe dish. Cook on High for 1 minute at a time, stirring in between, until the nuts begin to smell toasted and turn crisp. This will take from 2–6 minutes, depending on the type of nuts you are toasting and how powerful your microwave is.

3

2

4

CHOCOLATE CREAM PIE WITH PECAN NUT PASTRY

Pecan nuts, plain chocolate and coconut cream are the key ingredients in this rich and tempting dessert. The mouthwatering pastry is made from pecan nuts, sugar and butter.

SERVES: 12   **PREP TIME:** 45 mins, plus cooling & chilling   **COOK TIME:** 15 mins

INGREDIENTS

PASTRY

175 g/6 oz pecan nut pieces

50 g/1¾ oz sugar

55 g/2 oz butter, melted

FILLING

135 g/4¾ oz sugar

35 g/1¼ oz cornflour

½ tsp salt

4 large egg yolks

750 ml/1¼ pints almond milk

1 tsp vanilla extract

115 g/4 oz plain chocolate, 70% cocoa solids, melted

85 g/3 oz plain chocolate, 85% cocoa solids, melted

TOPPING

200 ml/7 fl oz canned coconut cream (chilled in the refrigerator overnight)

1 tbsp sugar

1 tsp vanilla extract

1. To make the pastry, preheat the oven to 200°C/400°F/ Gas Mark 6.

2. Put the nuts and sugar into a food processor and pulse until the nuts are finely chopped. Add the butter and pulse to combine. Turn out the mixture into a 23-cm/9-inch pie dish and press it evenly over the base and halfway up the side of the dish. Bake in the oven for about 15 minutes until light brown. Remove and cool the dish on a wire rack.

3. Meanwhile for the filling, put the sugar, cornflour, salt and egg yolks into a medium-sized saucepan and stir to combine. Place over a medium–high heat and add the almond milk in a thin stream, whisking constantly. Bring just to the boil, then immediately reduce the heat to low and cook, whisking constantly, for a further minute, or until the mixture thickens. Push the mixture through a fine-meshed sieve, then stir in the vanilla extract and melted chocolate. Cover with clingfilm, pressing it onto the surface of the mixture to prevent a film forming, and chill in the refrigerator for at least 2 hours.

4. Spoon the chilled filling into the pastry case, cover with clingfilm and chill for at least 4 hours or overnight.

5. To make the topping, open the can of coconut milk and carefully scoop out the thick cream at the top. Using a hand-held electric mixer with a whisk attachment, beat the coconut cream with the sugar for 8–10 minutes until it holds stiff peaks. Add the vanilla extract and beat to incorporate. Spoon the whipped cream on top of the pie and chill in the refrigerator for at least 2 hours. Serve chilled.

per serving: 372 Kcals / 27.1g fat / 10.8g sat fat / 29.7g carbs / 21.6g sugars / 3.5g fibre / 4g protein / 0.4g salt

BROWN SUGAR WALNUT CAKE

This simple but enticing cake is studded with crunchy toasted walnuts and benefits from a deep, caramel-like flavour and a deliciously chewy brown sugar crust.

SERVES: 12　　**PREP TIME:** 15 mins　　**COOK TIME:** 1 hour 10 mins

INGREDIENTS

10 g/¼ oz butter, for greasing

280 g/10 oz plain flour

½ tsp baking powder

½ tsp salt

440 g/15¾ oz soft light brown sugar

50 g/1¾ oz granulated sugar

225 g/8 oz butter, at room temperature

1 tbsp vanilla extract

4 eggs

175 ml/6 fl oz milk

60 g/2¼ oz walnuts, chopped

1. Preheat the oven to 180°C/350°F/Gas Mark 4 and grease a 2.4-litre/4-pint ring tin.

2. Put the flour, baking powder and salt into a medium-sized bowl and mix to combine.

3. Put the brown sugar, granulated sugar and butter into a separate bowl and beat with a hand-held electric mixer for 4 minutes, or until pale and fluffy. Add the vanilla extract and mix to incorporate. Add the eggs, one at a time, beating well after each addition.

4. Add half the flour mixture and half the milk to the wet mixture and mix until just incorporated. Add the remaining flour and milk and mix until incorporated. Add the nuts and mix again until they are just incorporated.

5. Transfer the batter to the prepared tin and bake in the preheated oven for 1 hour–1 hour 10 minutes, or until a skewer inserted into the middle of the cake comes out clean. Turn out the cake onto a wire rack and leave to cool completely before serving.

per serving: 449 Kcals / 21.4g fat / 11.2g sat fat / 59.6g carbs / 40.9g sugars / 1g fibre / 5.9g protein / 0.7g salt

3

4

5

HONEYED CARROT & PECAN SQUARES

This cake is packed with vitamin A-boosting carrots, vitamin B- and mineral-boosting wheatgerm and energy-boosting wholemeal flour. Who thought healthy ingredients could taste so good?

MAKES: 15   **PREP TIME:** 25 mins   **COOK TIME:** 35 mins

INGREDIENTS

3 eggs

150 ml/5 fl oz virgin olive oil

115 g/4 oz light muscovado sugar

5 tbsp set honey

175 g/6 oz wholemeal plain flour

4 tbsp wheatgerm

2 tsp baking powder

2 tsp ground ginger

grated zest of 1 orange

1¼ tsp ground mixed spice

175 g/6 oz carrots, coarsely grated

55 g/2 oz pecan nuts, broken into pieces

FROSTING

115 g/4 oz Greek-style natural yogurt

150 g/5½ oz cream cheese or mascarpone

1. Preheat the oven to 180°C/350°F/Gas Mark 4. Line a small non-stick roasting tin with a base measurement of 18 x 28 cm/7 x 11 inches with baking paper, snipping into the corners diagonally then pressing the paper into the tin so that both the base and sides are lined.

2. Crack the eggs into a large bowl, add the oil, sugar and 4 tablespoons of honey and whisk until smooth. Put the flour, wheatgerm and baking powder in a small bowl, then add the ginger, most of the orange zest and 1 teaspoon of mixed spice and stir. Add the dry ingredients to the egg mixture and whisk again until smooth. Add the carrots and most of the pecans and stir.

3. Spoon the mixture into the prepared tin and spread it into an even layer. Bake for 30–35 minutes, or until well risen and a skewer comes out cleanly when inserted into the centre of the cake.

4. Remove the cake from the tin, peel off the baking paper and turn out onto a wire rack. Leave to cool.

5. To make the frosting, put the yogurt, cream cheese and remaining 1 tablespoon of honey and ¼ teaspoon of mixed spice into a bowl and beat together until smooth. Spread the frosting over the cake, then sprinkle with the remaining pecans and orange zest. Cut it into 15 squares and serve.

per square: 294 Kcals / 20g fat / 5.3g sat fat / 25.8g carbs / 14.9g sugars / 2.4g fibre / 5.3g protein / 0.5g salt

PISTACHIO ICE CREAM

Made in an electric ice-cream maker with no dairy and no processed sugar, this is a feel-good treat. Creamy coconut milk and almond milk are sweetened with dates and the earthy pistachio nuts and almond extract give the ice cream an exotic and irresistible flavour.

SERVES: 6   **PREP TIME:** 10 mins   **COOK TIME:** none

INGREDIENTS

75 g/2¾ oz unsalted pistachio nuts, shelled

350 ml/12 fl oz coconut milk

350 ml/12 fl oz almond milk

8–10 Medjool dates, stoned

1 tsp vanilla extract

½ tsp almond extract

1. Put the nuts and about 125 ml/4 fl oz of the coconut milk into a food processor and process to a smooth paste.

2. Put the remaining coconut milk, the almond milk, dates, vanilla extract and almond extract into a blender. Whizz on high speed for 3–5 minutes, until puréed. Add the pistachio paste and process until well combined.

3. Transfer the mixture to the chilled container of an electric ice-cream maker and freeze according to the manufacturer's instructions. The ice cream can be served immediately, or you can transfer it to a freezer-proof container and freeze overnight for a more solid consistency.

per serving: 195 Kcals / 7.5g fat / 1.8g sat fat / 31.6g carbs / 25.9g sugars / 4g fibre / 3.5g protein / 0.1g salt

SUMMER FRUIT CRUMBLE

Here you'll find no less than three types of nuts combined in this delicious crumble topping, covering the warming, sweet melange of tree and bush fruits, ranging from nectarines and plums to blackberries and cherries.

SERVES: 8   **PREP TIME:** 40 mins, plus soaking and chilling   **COOK TIME:** 15 mins

INGREDIENTS

FILLING

55 g/2 oz soft light brown sugar

1 tbsp lemon juice

1½ tsp cornflour

½ tsp vanilla extract

pinch of salt

180 g/6¼ oz each nectarines, apricots, plums blackberries and cherries, stoned and sliced

TOPPING

35 g/1¼ oz toasted unsalted pecan nuts

35 g/1¼ oz walnuts

35 g/1¼ oz almonds

165 g/5¾ oz soft light brown sugar

40 g/1½ oz rolled oats

40 g/1½ oz plain flour

pinch of salt

85 g/3 oz chilled unsalted butter

1. Heat the oven to 220°C/425°F/Gas Mark 7.

2. To make the filling, put the sugar, lemon juice, cornflour, vanilla extract and salt into a large bowl and stir to mix well. Add the fruit and gently toss to coat. Transfer the fruit mixture to a 23-cm/9-inch pie dish or baking dish and spread in an even layer.

3. To make the topping, put the pecan nuts, walnuts, almonds, sugar, oats, flour and salt into a food processor and pulse to combine. Add the butter and pulse until the mixture clumps into pea-sized pieces. Spread over the fruit in an even layer.

4. Bake in the preheated oven for 20–25 minutes until the topping is crisp and brown. Remove from the oven and leave to cool on a wire rack for 30 minutes before serving. Serve warm.

> **TIP:** *A crunchy, nutty topping crowns a mixture of the season's most delicious fruit. Serve with a scoop of vanilla ice cream or a dollop of whipped cream.*

per serving: 484 Kcals / 23.7g fat / 8.3g sat fat / 67.2g carbs / 49.8g sugars / 6.1g fibre / 6g protein / 0.5g salt

RASPBERRY RICOTTA CHEESECAKE

Traditionally cheesecakes have a crushed biscuit base, but this granola-style base is packed with protein-filled nuts and cholesterol lowering oats.

SERVES: 8   **PREP TIME:** 40 mins   **COOK TIME:** 15mins, plus chilling

INGREDIENTS

1 tbsp virgin olive oil, to grease

25 g/1 oz unsalted butter

1 tbsp virgin olive oil

6 tbsp maple syrup

40 g/1½ oz porridge oats

40 g/1½ oz unblanched almonds, roughly chopped

40 g/1½ oz unblanched hazelnuts, roughly chopped

finely grated zest of ¼ unwaxed lemon, to decorate

8 tsp maple syrup, for drizzling

TOPPING

4 tbsp cold water

2½ tsp powdered gelatine

250 g/9 oz ricotta cheese

250 g/9 oz mascarpone cheese

250 g/9 oz natural yogurt

finely grated zest and juice of 1 unwaxed lemon

150 g/5½ oz raspberries

1. To make the base, preheat the oven to 160°C/325°F/ Gas Mark 3. Brush a 23-cm/9-inch diameter round non-stick springform tart tin with a little oil. Put the butter, oil and 2 tablespoons of maple syrup in a saucepan over a medium–low heat until the butter has melted. Remove the pan from the heat and stir in the oats and nuts.

2. Tip the mixture into the prepared tin and press down into an even layer with the back of a fork. Bake for 15 minutes, or until golden, then leave to cool.

3. To make the topping, spoon the water into a small heatproof bowl, then sprinkle the gelatine over the top, making sure all the powder is absorbed. Soak for 5 minutes. Place the bowl over a saucepan of gently simmering water until you have a clear liquid.

4. Put the ricotta, mascarpone and yogurt in a bowl, spoon in the remaining 4 tablespoons of maple syrup and whisk until smooth. Mix in the lemon zest and juice, then gradually whisk in the gelatine mixture. Add half the raspberries and crush them into the mixture with a fork.

5. Spoon the topping onto the base, smooth the surface and sprinkle with the remaining raspberries. Cover the cheesecake and chill for 4–6 hours, or until set.

6. To serve, run a knife around the edge of the tin, release the side and slide the cheesecake onto a serving plate. Decorate with the remaining lemon zest, cut into wedges and drizzle with extra maple syrup.

per serving: 389 Kcals / 29.3g fat / 14.3g sat fat / 22.9g carbs / 14.1g sugars / 3.2g fibre / 11g protein / 0.2g salt

INDEX